TEEN LIFE™

FREQUENTLY ASKED QUESTIONS ABOUT

Financial Literacy

Mary-Lane
Kamberg

ROSEN
PUBLISHING®
New York

For Rachel

Published in 2011 by The Rosen Publishing Group, Inc.
29 East 21st Street, New York, NY 10010

Library of Congress Cataloging-in-Publication Data

Kamberg, Mary-Lane, 1948–
Frequently asked questions about financial literacy / Mary-Lane Kamberg.—1st ed.
    p. cm.—(FAQ: teen life)
Includes bibliographical references and index.
ISBN 978-1-4488-1327-8 (library binding)
1. Finance, Personal—Juvenile literature. 2. Financial literacy—Juvenile literature. I. Title.
HG179.K356 2011
332.024—dc22

                                                    2010018500

Manufactured in the United States of America

CPSIA Compliance Information: Batch #W11YA: For further information, contact Rosen Publishing, New York, New York, at 1-800-237-9932.

Contents

Chapter one

WHAT SHOULD I DO WITH MY MONEY?

Your grandmother sends you a birth-day check. Your parents give you an allowance. You get a paycheck from a part-time job. Your great uncle leaves you money in his will. You win the lottery!

Wherever you get your money, you have financial decisions to make. Will you head for the mall and buy a new DVD? Save it to buy a laptop computer, prom dress, or cell phone? Or save it for major purchases like a car or college? Will you give some to charity?

If you want to make good financial decisions, make a plan for your money. And stick to it!

First, establish an emergency fund. For adults with full-time jobs, an emergency fund should be enough to cover all living expenses for three to six months. If you're a student with a part-time job, put away about three months' worth of your paychecks. This money should only be used in case of a real emergency—for

Financial goal-setting starts with a list of things you need or want. Separate the items according to short-term or long-term goals, and plan two separate savings options.

instance, if you lose your job, become sick and can't work (or earn any money), or your car needs unexpected repairs. Your emergency fund will let you continue your budget for three months. That means you have about three months to find a new job, or three months to refill your emergency fund.

Good money management starts with setting goals. And that starts with a list of things you need or want. Include everything you would like to have or do. Your list might include such items as the latest computer game, new shoes, a movie date, a spring break trip to Florida, a car, a new fragrance, or a college education. Once you have your list, put it in order.

Divide items into three groups: spending money, short-term goals, and long-term goals. You may consider adding a fourth group: charity. That's money you give to support your place of worship or favorite nonprofit organization. Within each group, rank the items in order of what is most important to you.

Spending money is for things that you can buy or do right away. These items usually have lower prices than those in the other groups. For example, spending money goes for gasoline, iTunes downloads, a cheeseburger and fries, a new shirt, or birthday gifts for friends. Short-term goals are items that may take a few weeks or months to save for, but the prices are low enough that you can save the money in less than a year. Examples include a camera, sound system, winter coat, and basketball shoes. Long-term goals are items that will take more than a year to save for: a motorcycle, a high-definition television, or a study-abroad year in France.

When you make your list, be sure your short-term and long-term goals include only items that are important to you. That way, you will be more likely to follow your savings plan. It's tempting to use all your money for spending right away. But if you have set your sights on products or activities that you really want, you will resist the temptation to spend money meant for those goals.

A budget is a plan for using your money. One way to divide your plan is to set aside one-third of it for each of the three groups. Some financial planners recommend that adults who have living expenses like rent and electric and heating bills save only about 10 percent of their earnings. The actual amount you set aside as savings is up to you. What's important is getting in the habit of saving.

How Can I Save When I Spend?

Once you have a budget, you're on your way to good money management. But there's more to money than knowing how much to spend or save. A recent FIND/SVP survey of three hundred teens reveals that teenagers place strong emphasis on getting value for their money.

When you spend money, try to get good value for each purchase. Value doesn't always mean the lowest price. Value is getting your money's worth—paying a fair price for goods or services. For example, a higher-priced laptop may be more useful for a longer time than a lower-priced one. But more expensive isn't always better. You might not need the advanced technology of a top-of-the-line computer.

One way to judge an item's value is to figure out how many hours you would have to work to earn the amount of money it costs. For instance, if a prom dress costs $480 and you make $8 an hour, it would take sixty hours to earn the money for that dress ($480 ÷ $8 = 60). Do you like it that much?

Another way to judge an item's value is to guess how often you will use that item. Most girls wear a prom dress only once. On the other hand, a student will use a laptop every day. If you figure the cost per use, you can make a good decision.

You can save money in other ways. If an item is on sale for 50 percent off (not uncommon at end-of-season sales), you will get a $50 pair of jeans for $25. If an item you want isn't on sale, ask a salesclerk if it's likely to go on sale soon. If it is, it's probably worth waiting for. Many items are seasonal, and they go on sale at the end of the season. For example, bathing suits go on sale at the end of summer, and you can find good sales on boots at the end of winter. If an item that you want is no longer there when the sale starts, you'll likely find something similar at a good price. However, sales can be deceiving. The low prices may

Save money when you shop by buying items on sale. Winter boots often go on sale as spring approaches but while there is still enough cold weather to wear them.

tempt you to buy more than you really need. Don't spend money that you're saving for other things.

When you shop, use a list. Buy only the items on that list. If you see something you would like to have, put it on your list for a future shopping trip.

Using retailers' coupons is another way to save. Retailers of clothing, electronics, and other items send coupons through the mail or electronically, especially during holiday shopping times. When using the Internet, you can enter the name of a store and then the word "coupon" to find printable coupons online. Some stores offer special prices to frequent customers. If you often shop at the same store, ask if there is a rewards program. If so, sign up for it! You could get discounts or gift cards for future purchases.

Retailers aren't the only places to shop. You'll find treasures at great prices at stores that sell used books, music, DVDs, and clothes. In some stores, you can offer a lower amount than the price on the tag. You can always buy the item at the asking price if the clerk says no. But if the answer is yes, you'll walk away with money in your pocket. Negotiating also works at some retailers. Give it a try!

If you prefer new items, buy generic brands in place of designer labels. It's easy to get caught up in fashion fads. But you will get more for your money if you bypass labels that add prestige without added quality.

Finally, before you shop, compare prices at Web-based retailers. You may save money buying online. Be sure to add the shipping and handling costs to your price comparisons. And remember to look for shipping discounts in online coupons.

Where Should I Keep My Money?

Spending money is meant to be spent. You need easy access to it. Keeping it in a wallet or piggy bank makes sense. But it may be tempting to spend cash that you keep on you. Plus, it's at risk for loss to theft, fire, or another disaster.

Instead, put your spending money in a checking account tied to a debit card. A debit card is a great way to avoid carrying cash. It's good for online shopping, and you can pay at the pump for gasoline. When you write a check or use the card, the bank takes the money out of your account and transfers it to the account of the person or business you paid.

Keep track of your deposits (the money you put in), withdrawals (the money you take out), and balance (what you have left). Never write a check or make a debit card purchase for more than you have. If you do, the bank will not pay the amount.

Never write a check or make a debit card purchase for more money than you have in your account. An overdraft costs you bank fees. You might even be prosecuted.

Instead, the check goes back to the store or person you wrote it to. This is called bouncing a check.

Bouncing a check will cost you. The bank charges an overdraft fee that can range from about $20 to more than $35 for each check that you bounce. You must then take cash to the store or person to pay for the bad check. Most stores charge a fee of another $15 or more. That's a lot to pay for a math mistake! If you accidentally bounce too many checks (or do it on purpose), you can be arrested and prosecuted for fraud. Fraud is deception for personal gain. The deception is you giving the impression that you have enough money in your account when you really don't. The gain is what you buy with the bad check.

Most teens open their first accounts at their parents' bank or credit union. (A credit union is a nonprofit financial institution like a bank but owned by its members.) Sometimes a different one is a better choice for you. Compare services offered by others. Do they have student accounts? What's the minimum deposit? Are minimum balances required? What fees do they charge? What services do they offer?

Today, most banks offer online banking. (In fact, some banks are virtual—they exist only on the Web.) Other services that appeal to teens include text-message banking. Account holders can text to check balances, pay bills, and transfer money from one account to another. Some checking accounts offer rewards programs that give you free cash, merchandise, or travel credits, or let you donate money to a nonprofit organization.

CHAPTER TWO

HOW CAN MY MONEY GROW?

Financial planners like to say, "Let your money work for you." Your money can make money if you invest in cash, bonds, or stocks.

Savings accounts are safe and easy investments in cash. If the bank is robbed or goes broke, the Federal Deposit Insurance Corporation (FDIC) pays the amount you had up to a limit for each account. Insurance administered by the federal National Credit Union Administration (NCUA) covers most credit unions. Some credit unions are insured by a private company called American Share Insurance (ASI).

When you put money in a savings account, the bank or credit union lends some of the money it holds. It charges interest to the person who borrows it. The interest is the profit the bank makes. The bank pays you a percentage of its profit. The money you get is also called

When you open a savings account, be sure you understand the interest rate the bank will pay you, as well as how the bank computes the amount.

interest. Interest paid to deposit accounts is tied to loan rates. For example, if the bank charges 4 percent interest on auto loans, the interest it pays on savings accounts might be 0.1 percent. If loan rates are low, savings account rates are low, too. As loan interest rates rise, so do savings account rates.

When you open an interest-bearing account, ask how the interest is figured. One way is called simple interest. That means you earn interest only on the money that you deposit. With compound interest, each time interest is added up (compounded), the amount is figured on the total of what you deposited, plus the interest you have earned so far. For a savings account, you want compound interest. Your money grows faster.

A savings account is a good place to keep money for short-term goals. Put money for long-term goals in a higher-interest investment like a money market savings account (if you have the minimum deposit) or a certificate of deposit (CD). A CD is not a musical recording! It's a loan you make to a bank. You agree to leave your money there for a set period of time (often three months to six years). If you take out the money before the time is up, you pay a penalty and may earn no interest at all.

Isn't Investing Risky Business?

You won't lose money with insured savings accounts. But investing in securities, the term for stocks and bonds, is a different story. None is insured like a bank account. You can lose some or all of your money.

Despite the risk, securities can earn more interest than a savings account or CD. Over time, the stock market offers the best returns. According to *Standard & Poor's Guide to Understanding Personal Finance*, stocks in general have earned more than other types of investments over every fifteen-year period since 1926. (This history applies only to the entire market, not necessarily to any individual stock.)

Still, never put money you need at risk. Don't invest in securities until:

- You pay all your bills each month.
- Your emergency fund covers at least three months.
- You have met your short-term and long-term savings goals.

You may hear investors refer to "Wall Street" or the "market" when talking about buying and selling stocks. A stock market or exchange is where companies offer a share of ownership. In exchange, you get a share of the profits. The New York Stock Exchange (NYSE) is sometimes called the Big Board. It's the main stock exchange in the United States. Two others are the National Association of Securities Dealers Automated Quotation System (NASDAQ) and the American Stock Exchange (AMEX). Each exchange trades for different lists of companies.

The Standard & Poor's 500 (S&P 500) tells you how the market is doing. It's an index of the average price of the shares in the five hundred largest companies in the United States. You can also check the Dow Jones Industrial Average, which averages thirty-four American companies. The NASDAQ Composite tracks that market. If a stock exchange's average price is rising over time, it is called a bull market. If it's losing value, it's a bear market.

When you buy stock, you become part owner in a company. You share the profits. When you invest, your strategy can emphasize either the profit that the stock earns or the market value of a share. Investors looking for income from their stocks buy growth stocks. These are stocks with above-average profits. Those who tend toward the "buy low, sell high" philosophy buy value stocks. They hope to make money by selling shares for a price higher than they paid for it.

A stock's market value is the price that someone is willing to pay for something. The stock market is an auction house. Perhaps you've seen people on a trading floor on the news or in

Investing in the stock market means becoming part owner of a company. You earn a share of the company's profits—if it makes a profit.

a movie. During a trading day, traders bid on certain stocks at certain prices. The price goes up and down during the day. The price depends on the ever-changing demand for the stock and the supply of stock for sale.

Growth and value investing are related. The value of a stock depends on its chance of making a profit. Suppose you pay $100 for a share of stock. The company does well. You earn dividends. The more the company makes, the more investors want to own part of it. They will pay more than $100 for a share. That drives up the price of a share.

If it rises to $150, your investment is worth $50 more than what you paid for it. On the other hand, if the company loses money, you won't get any money. Some investors will want to sell. If a lot of people want to sell, the price goes down. Suppose it sells for $90 per share. The value of your investment goes down. If you sell your share when its value is $90, you lose $10 on your investment. However, you do not make or lose money until the day you actually sell the stock.

No one can accurately predict what will happen. However, you can pay attention to current events that can have an impact on the industry and company you invest in. You can also watch for news about specific companies. Read press releases on their Web sites. Perhaps a company is about to release a new product. Or you may hear that customers might file a lawsuit against it. These kinds of news affect a stock's value. Research and analysis will help you decide which stocks to buy and when to sell them. You can do it yourself. Or you can pay an experienced financial adviser to do it for you.

If you're interested in the stock market, you can play online stock market games to learn more. Some schools have clubs where you can pretend to invest in stock and measure your results. For the real thing, your parents can invest for you until you turn eighteen, the minimum age for owning stock.

What Are Bonds?

A bond is a loan that you make to a corporation, organization, or federal, state, or city government. A manufacturer might need money to buy modern equipment. A school district might borrow money to build a new high school. They issue a bond.

You buy a bond in the bond market for a specific period of time. The issuer promises to pay you back at the end of that time, usually with a set amount of interest. You have no ownership in the company. The end of the loan period is called the maturity date. The interest paid at maturity is called the yield. The yield is your profit on your investment. Bonds may mature in a matter of months or years, perhaps many years. The Walt Disney Company and others have issued bonds that mature in one hundred years. Safra Republic Holdings, a company in Luxembourg, issued bonds in 1997 that mature in 2997, a full one thousand years later.

If you buy a bond, you take a chance that the issuer might default on the bond. Default means that the issuer can't pay you back at the maturity date. The size of your risk depends on the type of bonds that you buy. Financial experts consider bonds issued by the federal government to be the safest. If the govern-

When you buy a U.S. Savings Bond, you are lending money to the federal government. Experts consider these bonds to be among the safest bond investments.

ment can't pay you, it can tax citizens to raise the money. There is almost no chance that the government will default. U.S. Savings Bonds and U.S. Treasury Bonds are examples of this type of bond. Other bonds include municipal, corporate, mortgage-backed or asset-backed securities, and international bonds—each with its own risk and possible reward.

You invest in stocks or bonds through an account at a bank, insurance company, investment company, brokerage house, or mutual fund. In a mutual fund, investors put all their money together. For a fee, a professional mutual fund manager buys and sells stocks and/or bonds based on his or her research and expertise.

In other cases, you pay a fee based on what you buy or sell. Be sure to include the fee when you consider selling. The fee can be more than you stand to make on the sale. For example, if a stock is selling at $10 more than you paid for it, you might think about selling. But if you must pay an $8 fee for the sale, you make only $2. You might want to hold the stock a little longer.

A good investment strategy is to invest for the long-term and not worry about daily changes in stock prices. Another good idea is to invest in a mix of cash, bonds, and stocks. Buy stocks or bonds from different companies; this practice is called diversification. If you diversify, you spread the risk around. You might not make as much, but you reduce your chances of losing all your money.

chapter
three

HOW DO I BORROW MONEY?

Sometimes you need or want something so expensive that you cannot save enough in time to buy it. For big purchases like a car or college education, you may need to borrow money. You can do that through credit cards or other loans.

A credit card looks like a debit or gift card. However, it works differently. When you use a credit card, you are taking out a loan. You have to pay it back—with interest. Credit cards are useful tools. They help you establish a credit history, and they are priceless when your car breaks down between paydays or in another emergency. (Remember, seeing a great pair of shoes at the mall is not an emergency!)

Credit cards also let you take advantage of a sale price on something you were already saving to buy. If you're saving for a new guitar, for example, and it goes on sale,

It's easy to spend too much when you're using a credit card. The best practice is to charge only the amount you can pay in full each month.

charge it. You'll save money—but only if you use the savings you've accumulated to pay part of the bill. And pay the rest as soon as possible. If you don't pay the credit card bill in full each month, finance charges can add up to more money than you saved.

Overspending with credit cards is tempting and easy. Never use one to buy something you know you can't afford. The same goes for impulse purchases. Adopt a cash-only rule for things that you eat or use up right away. If you won't still have it when the bill comes, don't charge it on a credit card. You can get yourself in trouble if you can't pay the bill in full each month.

You can get in more trouble—and higher debt—if you can't make even the minimum monthly payment on a credit card. Minimum monthly payments are just that: the minimum. In fact, a minimum payment is almost entirely interest, or finance charges. Very little goes toward paying down your balance. If you make an additional purchase, the interest multiplies. It can take years to pay off the balance.

To get a credit card, simply fill out an application at a bank or online. Your first card will likely have a fairly low credit limit. A credit limit is the highest amount that your balance can be. Before you have established a credit history, you may have a hard time getting your first card. One way to get one is to open a secured card. A secured card may be one that your parents guarantee. (The person who guarantees the card is the cosigner. If you don't pay, the cosigner must pay.)

Another secured card is tied to a savings account. Your savings balance is your credit limit. You get billed for the purchases you make. You leave the money in the savings account and pay the bill from other income. If you don't pay your credit card bill as agreed, the bank can take the money from your account. However, if you pay your bill on time over several months, the bank may issue you a traditional card. You'll still have the money in the savings account.

Not all credit cards are created equally. Before you accept one, compare your costs. The first thing to know is the finance charge you'll pay on what you owe. Be sure to find out if the rate is a special "introductory" rate that expires in a matter of months and morphs into a higher rate. Ask if there is a different interest rate for cash advances on the card. Many credit card companies charge more for a cash advance than for a purchase. The interest is very high. Avoid using a credit card to borrow cash this way.

Also, compare the credit limit you're offered and the grace period. The grace period is the time that you have to pay off the balance without owing interest. Generally, if you pay the entire bill every month, you won't owe interest. However, you may have to pay an annual fee. If your payment is late, or if you charge more than your credit limit, you will pay high penalties. You may even see your interest rate go up.

Be responsible with credit card purchases. A good rule of thumb is to keep your credit card debt lower than 15 percent of your annual take-home pay.

Where Else Can I Borrow Money?

A credit card is the most expensive way to borrow money. For big purchases like a car or college tuition, you will pay less

The best way to buy a car is with cash. If you must borrow money, make the largest down payment you can afford. Be sure you understand the loan terms.

interest if you take out a loan. If you need to buy a car or pay for college tuition, save as much as you can toward the purchase. Then consider applying for a loan. The money you pay for the money you borrow is (again) called interest.

The important features of a loan include the amount you borrow, the interest rate, the time you have to pay it back, and the amount of each payment. In general, the longer you have to pay the balance, the lower the interest rate. (However, you will pay more interest in the long run because you pay for a longer time.) The shorter the time you need to pay back the loan and the higher the payments, the less total interest you'll pay. Never borrow more than you have to. Use your long-term savings to make a down payment on the purchase.

Remember the interest you earn on savings accounts and other investments? In those situations, others owe you money. They pay you interest for using your money. And you want the interest to be compounded.

With a loan, the practice is reversed. When you use someone else's money, you pay interest. You want a loan with simple interest.

If you fail to pay back the loan as agreed, you default on the loan. What happens next depends on whether your loan is unsecured or secured. An unsecured loan is one that is not guaranteed with property. Unsecured loans have a higher interest rate. The lender may require a cosigner.

A secured loan is one that requires you to put up property. This property is called collateral. If you default, you lose your property. The most common secured loan is a car loan. If you don't pay, you lose your car.

The best way to buy a car is with cash. Put savings in a long-term investment until you have enough. If you need to take out a car loan, make the highest down payment you can. Ask for the shortest-term loan that you can afford. Put any extra money you get toward paying off the loan early. A word of warning: never risk losing your car by using it as collateral for a title loan. A title loan is a high-interest loan for quick cash. The loan company holds onto your car title until you pay off the loan. If you can't repay, you lose your car.

Before you borrow money for education expenses, learn how much you can expect to earn if you work in your field of study. Figure out how many years you'll have to work to repay the debt. Borrow the least you need. Apply for scholarships and grants that do not have to be repaid. For loans, see if part or all of the balance will be erased if you work in a certain job for a length of time (also known as loan forgiveness).

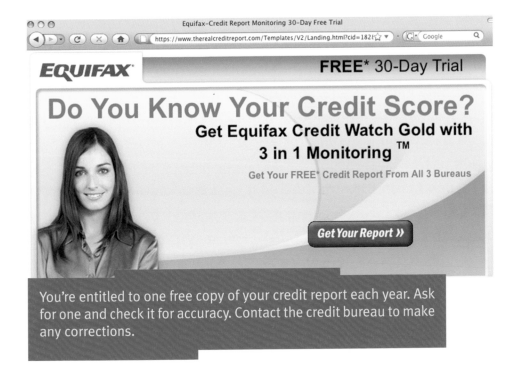

You're entitled to one free copy of your credit report each year. Ask for one and check it for accuracy. Contact the credit bureau to make any corrections.

What's a Credit History?

When you open your first bank account, credit card, or loan, your credit history begins. The three major credit agencies in the United States are Equifax, Experian, and TransUnion. These bureaus collect information about you. This information includes balances that you owe to banks, finance companies, credit card companies, and online merchants. It also includes whether or not you pay your bills on time. If not, they record how late you are. They know when you apply for new credit cards or loans. They also know where you work, your Social Security number, and your birthday. In short, when it comes to you and money, these credit bureaus know everything. They share this information with companies or banks you apply to for credit cards, other loans, or even jobs. Credit information services assign a credit score between 300 and 850, based on your history. The better your history, the higher your score. The higher your score, the more likely you'll qualify for a loan and the lower interest rate you'll pay.

A good credit history makes it easier to get a job or borrow for major purchases like a car or a house. A bad credit history will cramp your style in a hurry. You may not get a new credit card or loan. If you do, you're likely to pay a higher interest rate than someone with a good history. You may even be turned down for a job. Know what your credit report says about you. If you ask, these companies must give you one free copy of your credit report each year. Ask for it. Look it over. If you see errors, contact the agency to make corrections.

Ten Great Questions to Ask a Financial Expert

1 What's a budget and why do I need one?

2 How can I get the most for my money?

3 What fees can I expect from using a checking account?

4 What should I do if I find a mistake on my credit report?

5 What's the difference between simple and compound interest?

6 What's the difference between value and growth investing?

7 What's a bear market?

8 How does my credit history affect me?

9 I'm young—why do I have to pay for Medicare?

10 What's identity theft?

chapter four

WHAT SHOULD I KNOW ABOUT TAXES AND INSURANCE?

On your way to school, you may walk on sidewalks or ride on public streets patrolled by police officers. Perhaps you pass a park. Your country is protected by the military. At home, your trash is collected once a week. And if your house catches fire, you call 911 for help. Taxes pay for these types of services. And where do taxes come from? You.

The Sixteenth Amendment to the U.S. Constitution gives the government the authority to collect taxes. But you have a voice. Your representative in the U.S. Congress, state legislature, and city government helps decide how much taxes are. Let your representatives know your opinion on issues involving your money. Call, e-mail, or send a letter to their offices.

You likely already know about sales tax. You pay it when you buy a candy bar, belt, or any item. But if you've never had a job, you might be surprised to see your first

Elected representatives at city, state, and federal levels, like U.S. Representative John Garamendi of California, decide what to tax, tax rates, and what taxes pay for.

paycheck. The federal government collects money through the Federal Insurance Contribution Act (FICA). Your employer takes taxes out of what you earn. The employer pays an equal amount. FICA taxes go toward Social Security and Medicare. These federal programs pay for an income safety net and health care for older Americans and people with disabilities.

The federal government and most states also tax your income. Federal income tax is progressive. That means the more you make, the higher percentage of your money you pay.

In some cases, especially if you only work part-time and make little money over a year, you may not have to pay withholding taxes. (However, you are still responsible for FICA taxes.) In other words, you are exempt. When you take a job, you'll fill out a W-4 form. If you owed no federal tax the year before and earn less than a certain amount, the employer won't withhold income taxes.

At the end of the year, if taxes were withheld, your employer issues a W-2 form. If you owe tax or owe less than the amount withheld, you must file an income tax return with the Internal Revenue Service (IRS) by April 15 each year. If your employer withheld more money than you owe in taxes, you'll get a tax refund. (You have to file a return to get the money.) If the amount was too little, you have to pay the difference.

According to H&R Block, the top five ways that teens can make sure to get their first refund include:

- Keep good records.
- Increase the amount of money withheld from your first job if you have a second job.
- Be sure the IRS has your current address or file online using accurate bank account information for direct deposit.
- Carefully fill out your W-4 form. It tells your employer how much to withhold from your paychecks. The withholding allowances that you enter affect your refund or what you owe.
- Don't expect to itemize on your first return. That means donations to charity and other tax-deductible expenses won't reduce your taxable income.

You are responsible for other taxes, too. You pay personal property tax when you buy a car. When you buy gas for it, you pay gasoline tax. In the future, you might also pay real-estate tax, telephone tax, gift and estate tax, or even tax for owning a dog. The list seems endless! As you plan the use of your money, keep in mind the taxes that you will owe.

What Insurance Do I Need?

You crash into a truck at an intersection. You fall and break a leg. Someone steals your laptop. Your house catches fire. These types of events can cost you—a lot. How can you protect what you have? At least, how can you reduce your financial loss?

Insurance is a contract between you and an insurance company. Different types of insurance cover different situations. Car insurance protects you by paying (within limits) medical bills or damage you cause to another car or someone else's property in an accident. Health insurance pays part of your medical bills. Renters insurance covers your personal possessions when you rent an apartment or house. Homeowners insurance covers theft, as well as storm damage, fire, and other disasters. Life insurance helps your family replace your income if you die.

Teens have little need for most types of insurance. You're likely covered by your parents' health and homeowners or renters policies. But if you leave for college, your parents may need additional insurance for you. Ask them to contact their insurance agent and health care insurance provider. You won't need life insurance until someone (like a spouse or child) depends on your income. (But the younger and healthier you

Motor vehicle liability insurance pays for personal injury and property damage you cause to others. After an accident, an insurance adjuster will examine property damage to the victim's car.

are when you take out a policy, the less each payment—or premium—will be.)

However, if you drive, you need motor vehicle insurance. State laws require that all motor vehicles have bodily injury and property damage liability insurance. This type of insurance pays for medical bills, car repairs, and damage to other property if you're at fault in an accident. It protects you financially (up to certain limits) if the injured person sues you. Some states have no-fault laws. In these states, each person's insurance covers damage to his or her own car up to a specified limit.

Your state may also require personal injury protection to pay your own medical expenses, no matter who is at fault. What if you're in an accident with a driver who has no liability insurance? Uninsured motorist insurance covers your medical bills or damage to your vehicle.

If you drive a car that you paid for in full, those types of coverage might be all the vehicle insurance you need. However, if you use a car as collateral for a car loan, your lender will require collision and comprehensive insurance, too. These types of insurance protect the lender if you total your car and can't pay off the balance of the loan. (If you default and the lender takes your car, it won't be worth anything.) Collision insurance covers damage to your vehicle. Comprehensive insurance covers such other events as theft or damage from storms, fire, or other losses. Lenders require this coverage so that the property you use to get the loan holds its value.

Insurance rates are based on the company's chances of having to pay benefits. If you fall into a group that costs companies more money than other groups, you will pay more. It's not personal. It's all about the numbers. Insurance companies rely on information compiled by an actuary. An actuary is a person who estimates the risks of certain events happening—things like motor vehicle accidents, earthquakes, and death at certain ages. He or she compiles a table that helps insurance companies decide how much to charge customers for different types of insurance.

Your rate depends on your age, gender, and the geographic area where you live. Teen drivers have more traffic accidents than older drivers, so their rates are much higher than those for experienced drivers. Young males pay more than young females. Car insurance also costs more in areas that have a lot of accidents and areas with high theft rates. If you fall into one or more of these groups, you can't do much about it.

But your rates also depend on your driving record, the type of vehicle you have, and the number of miles you drive each year. You can control these issues. Do your best to avoid accidents and traffic tickets. Stay within speed limits. Obey other traffic laws. And never drive under the influence of alcohol or other drugs (even prescriptions). Don't eat or use your cell phone while driving. And never let yourself be distracted by texting. Minimize possible injury by always wearing a seat belt. Make your passengers do the same.

You can save money on car insurance in several ways. For teens, good grades may get you a discount. So will taking a driver's education class. Your credit history can also affect your rate—another reason to establish a good credit score.

Sports cars and SUVs cost the most to insure. So do models that are popular with thieves. Before you buy a car, check rates with your insurance agent.

Before you buy a car, call an insurance company. Find out which models have the lowest rates. Sports cars, those with a lot of horsepower, and big SUVs have the highest. Buy something that doesn't fall into those groups. You'll also pay more if the model you drive is popular with car thieves. However, you might get a discount if you install an antitheft device.

Buy all your insurance policies in one place. Some companies offer discounts to insure more than one car. Discounts also apply if the company covers homeowners or renters insurance. Measure the mileage to and from school and work. That way, you can estimate how much you drive. Drivers average about

15,000 miles (24,140 kilometers) per year. If you don't drive that much, you may qualify for a lower rate. Payment methods can save you money as well. Ask for a yearly policy instead of a six-month one. And let the company automatically take your payment from your checking account. (Be sure to subtract the withdrawal every month.)

Finally, you pay less if you choose a higher deductible. A deductible is the amount that you pay out of your own pocket before insurance pays your claim. For instance, if you have a $500 deductible, you pay the first $500 in damages. But a $1,000 deductible costs less. So set aside enough to pay the deductible if something happens. You'll get a lower rate.

Chapter five

WHAT ARE MY RIGHTS AND RESPONSIBILITIES?

When you begin using financial services of any kind, you have consumer protections and other rights. You also have responsibilities.

For example, if your credit card is lost or stolen, you're responsible only for a limited amount of money (about $50) that a thief charges on your card. Of course, you must report the card lost or stolen as soon as you realize it. So keep the phone number for your credit card issuer (or issuers) handy. But if you write a check for more than you have in your account, you're responsible for paying the penalty. And you may face criminal charges. Federal legislation defines your consumer rights.

Some of your rights stem from the federal Truth in Lending Act. When you borrow money, the lender must give you a truth-in-lending disclosure statement. The statement is a document that covers five basic areas:

1. **The annual percentage rate (APR).** The APR is your cost if you owe the money for one year. The total cost includes such information as finance charges, interest rates, and other fees. Some loans have a fixed rate. This means that the interest rate and the amount of the payment remain the same over the length of the loan. Other loans and some credit cards have adjustable rates. The interest rate changes according to market conditions. Your payment can go up or down. An adjustable rate loan can be dangerous. If your payment goes up, you might not be able to afford it.

2. **The total cost of the loan in dollars.** That's the dollar amount that the credit will cost you. This includes interest and any fees you pay as a condition of the loan.

3. **The total amount you are borrowing.**

4. **The total of the payments** (including interest and other fees) if you make them all as scheduled.

5. **The payment schedule.** The payment schedule breaks down how much interest and how much of the balance you pay in each payment. With some loans, such as home loans, the first several years of payments mostly go toward interest. Only a small percentage goes to pay off the balance. As the borrower gets to the end of the loan, a smaller percentage of each payment goes to interest and more goes to pay off the balance.

Install an antitheft device, and you may get a discount on your car insurance. Good grades, a driver's education class, and a good credit history can result in more savings.

Additional consumer protections are included in new credit card rules that went into effect in February 2010. The rules prevent companies from charging fees higher than 25 percent of your credit limit during the first year you have a credit card. They also can't raise interest rates on existing balances if you pay on time. They can't charge interest in a new month on the part of the balance

that you paid off the month before. And they can't charge penalty interest just because some of your payments on other bills are late.

Another change affects those between the ages of eighteen and twenty-one. In the past, many credit card companies were eager to issue cards to people in this age group. Many young

New credit card rules went into effect in 2010, making it harder for teens to get credit cards unless they have the ability to pay the bills.

consumers got caught in the credit card trap. They charged too many purchases and ran up high finance charges and penalties. Now, however, credit card companies must verify a young customer's ability to pay. They may also require a cosigner before issuing a card.

If a company makes changes that you don't agree with, you can cancel the card without paying the balance in full. In fact, you'll have five years to pay off the bill. The rules now let customers first apply payments to the part of the balance with the highest interest rate.

New statements show how many years it will take you to pay off the card if you make only the minimum payment each month. (You'll be shocked to see how long it is!) You'll also see the amount of payment you need to make if you want to pay off the balance in three years.

What Are My Responsibilities?

Once you reach the age of majority, you are legally considered an adult. You are responsible for your own actions. You have the legal capacity to be held to an agreement. If you sign a contract, you must do what you say you will do, such as make the payments on time. You must live up to your side of the bargain. That means the contract is binding. In financial affairs, you are responsible for debts in your name.

Each state decides its own age of majority. Most have chosen age eighteen or nineteen. The age of majority does not affect when you can vote, drink alcohol, or gamble. Other laws determine when you can do those things.

If a company lets a minor (someone younger than the age of majority) enter into a contract, the minor can get out of the obligation. That's why companies won't enter into contracts with you when you're underage unless you have a parent's consent. A minor cannot take out a car loan, for example. You cannot own stock. (A minor can, however, sign contracts for student loans.) If you try to take out a loan, a bank will require an adult cosigner. A minor can't legally marry or own a business. No one can hold you to these actions and decisions until you reach the age of majority.

Some teens think that the age of majority restricts them. In fact, it protects them. When you're still a minor, you can get out of a contract if a salesperson pushes you to buy or sign something that you later regret. You can't be held responsible for what you signed. But if you have legal capacity to sign a contract and it later turns out that you didn't understand what you signed, you must still pay what you agreed to pay. Ignorance of the contract terms is no excuse. So never sign an agreement that you don't understand. And never sign an agreement that you don't think you can follow through on.

Because you're responsible for debts in your name, be careful to protect your identity. The Federal Trade Commission (FTC) estimates that nine million Americans are victims of identity theft each year. Many of them are teens. Identity theft means that someone illegally uses your name, Social Security number, credit card number, or other personal information without your permission.

Identity thieves use your information to open credit card accounts, take out loans in your name, sign up for cell phone services and run up the bills, and other crimes. When these bills go unpaid, the bad payment record goes straight to your credit history. Worse, if the thief is arrested for something, the thief can use a fake driver's license with your information but his or her photo to identify himself or herself and arrange for bail. When the thief fails to appear in court, the judge could issue a warrant for your arrest.

Damages from identity theft can run into thousands of dollars. You likely won't know anything about your losses until unusual things happen. Charges you didn't make appear on your credit card statement. A bill collection agency calls you about an account you never opened. A bank turns you down for a loan. Or you're denied a job, among other surprises.

You can protect yourself by following the FTC's advice: deter, detect, defend. Deter means taking action to prevent or discourage identity thieves. Shred bank statements, credit card bills, and other financial documents before you throw them away. Keep your Social Security card in a safe place—not your wallet. Never use your Social Security number on your driver's license

Protect your identity! An identity theft ring arrested in New York cost consumers, banks, and retailers more than $1 million in just one year.

or to identify yourself when you cash a check. Keep all of your passwords secret.

Carry credit cards only when you go shopping. The rest of the time, keep them at home. Also keep a master list of all credit cards and the phone numbers where you report loss or theft. If you lose your entire wallet, you'll need the list to contact the companies right away. Also, never let anyone else use your credit card or know your credit card account number.

Never give out personal information over the phone or Internet. You can't be sure that the people you're talking with or e-mailing are who they say they are. For online shopping, be sure that the Web site is secure. Look for an "https" at the beginning of its address. Also look for a padlock icon.

Do your best to detect identity theft. Watch your credit card bill for charges you didn't make. Call your credit card company if you don't get a bill on time. (A thief may have changed the billing address to get your personal information.) If you get a bill from a company you don't do business with, contact it at once. Ask why you're turned down for a loan or other credit. Check your credit history at least once a year. Report anything that's incorrect or unusual.

Defend against identity theft by filing a police report. File another report with the Federal Trade Commission. Place a fraud alert on your credit reports by contacting Experian, TransUnion, or Equifax. The fraud alert warns businesses to follow certain steps before opening a new account in your name or making changes to one that you already have. Close any accounts the thief used, as well as any new accounts that he or she opened.

When it comes to financial matters, entering the real world can be a little scary. But if you're armed with basic knowledge of budgeting and money-saving practices, you're off to a good start. Establish a habit of saving as much as you can each time that money comes into your hands. And keep savings in a savings account instead of a piggy bank or wallet.

Never risk money that you need. Don't even think about investing until you've met other financial obligations. However, you can learn as much as possible about stocks and bonds. You'll be prepared when you reach that point. Pay whatever taxes you owe. Be sure to protect your money and property from loss. Know your rights and responsibilities. Safeguard your identity. These tips will keep you in good standing, and you'll have the financial freedom you need to do whatever you want to do.

Myths and Facts

I can use a credit card for my purchases because I can easily afford the minimum payment.

Fact ➡ If you pay only the minimum payment on a credit card, you are mostly paying finance charges. Very little goes toward paying off the balance. The longer you take to pay the debt, the more finance charges you'll pay.

Taking out high amounts of student loans for college is OK because I'll be able to pay them off when I get a full-time job.

Fact ➡ Before you take on student loan debt, look into the salary you can expect for a job in your field. Figure out how long it will take you to pay off the loans.

A bad credit history won't affect my chances of getting a job.

Fact ➡ Many employers check applicants' credit reports before deciding to hire them. A bad credit history can cost you a job.

Glossary

age of majority The age you are legally considered an adult.

bounce (a check) To write a check for more than you have in your account. The bank or other financial institution will return the check unpaid to the person you wrote the check to.

budget A plan for how you will spend your money.

collateral Property that secures a loan. If the borrower defaults, the lender keeps the property.

credit limit The highest amount that your balance can be.

deductible The amount an insured person pays before insurance covers a loss.

default Failure to pay a debt when it is due.

diversification Spreading investments among different companies or types of investments to reduce the risk of losing money.

fraud Deception for personal gain.

grace period The time you have to pay off a balance without owing interest.

growth stock Stock in a company that consistently earns above-average profits.

identity theft The theft and use of a name, Social Security number, credit card number, or other personal information for illegal purposes.

interest An amount paid as a percentage of the amount lent or borrowed.

market value The price a buyer is willing to pay for something.

maturity date The date that a bond comes due.

negotiating Bargaining for a lower price than a seller is asking.

overdraft fee The amount a bank or other financial institution charges as a penalty for writing a check or making a debit purchase for more than you have in your account.

premium The payment for an insurance policy.

value A fair price in exchange for goods or services.

value investing Buying stock in a company with the hope of making money when it is later sold at a higher price.

yield Interest earned on an investment in stocks, bonds, or mutual funds.

American Bankers Association Education Foundation

1120 Connecticut Avenue NW

Washington, DC 20036

(800) BANKERS (226-5377)

Web site: http://www.aba.com

The American Bankers Association Education Foundation
is a subsidiary of the American Bankers Association.
It offers two national financial education programs to
assist bankers in teaching personal finance skills to
children and young adults: "Teach Children to Save"
and "Get Smart About Credit."

Association for Financial Counseling and Planning Education

1500 W. Third Avenue, Suite 223

Columbus, OH 43212

(614) 485-9650

Web site: http://www.afcpe.org

The Association for Financial Counseling and Planning
Education is a nonprofit, professional organization dedi-
cated to educating, training, and certifying financial
counselors and educators.

Canadian Bankers Association

Box 348

Commerce Court West

199 Bay Street, 30th Floor

Toronto, ON M5L 1G2

Canada

(800) 263-0231

Web site: http://www.cba.ca

The Canadian Bankers Association is an advocacy group that
promotes policies that contribute to a sound banking system
and financial literacy among Canadians.

Council for Economic Education

122 East 42nd Street, Suite 2600

New York, NY 10168

(800) 338-1192

Web site: http://www.councilforeconed.org

The Council for Economic Education advocates for better
school-based economic and personal finance education. It
offers educational programs and teaching resources.

Financial Advisors Association of Canada

Advocis

390 Queens Quay West, Suite 209

Toronto, ON M5V 3A2

Canada

(800) 563-5822

Web site: http://www.advocis.ca

The Financial Advisors Association of Canada is a voluntary
professional association of financial advisers in Canada.

It communicates with government and the public about industry issues.

Institute for Financial Literacy
P.O. Box 1842
Portland, ME 04104-1842
(207) 879-0389
Web site: http://www.financiallit.org
The Institute for Financial Literacy is a nonprofit educational association that provides financial counseling and education to adults. It sets the National Standards for Adult Financial Literacy Education, maintains the Library of Personal Finance, and administers the Center for Financial Certifications and the Center for Consumer Financial Research.

Institute of Consumer Financial Education
P.O. Box 34070
San Diego, CA 92163
(619) 239-1401
Web site: http://www.financial-education-icfe.org
The Institute of Consumer Financial Education is a nonprofit public education organization that promotes saving, wise credit use, and investment.

Jump$tart Coalition for Personal Financial Literacy
919 18th Street NW, Suite 300
Washington, DC 20006

(888) 45-EDUCATE (338-2283)

Web site: http://www.jumpstartcoalition.org

Jump$tart is a national alliance of organizations dedicated to
improving financial education for kindergarten through
college-age youth to prepare them to make good financial
decisions for life.

National Youth Involvement Board

South Carolina Credit Union League

P.O. Box 1787

Columbia, SC 29202

(800) 235-4290

Web site: http://www.nyib.org

The National Youth Involvement Board provides information
about credit unions to young people through marketing
materials, leadership opportunities, alliances, and educational conferences.

Native Financial Education Coalition

First Nations Oweesta Corporation

1010 Ninth Street, Suite 3

Rapid City, SD 57701

(605) 342-3770

Web site: http://www.oweesta.org

The Native Financial Education Coalition is a group of local,
regional, and national organizations and government agencies that promote financial management skills in native
communities.

360 Degrees of Financial Literacy

American Institute of Certified Public Accountants

1211 Avenue of the Americas

New York, NY 10036

(888) 777-7077

Web site: http://www.aicpa.org

360 Degrees of Financial Literacy is a volunteer service of the American Institute of Certified Public Accountants. It helps children and adults understand personal finances and develop money management skills.

Web Sites

Due to the changing nature of Internet links, Rosen Publishing has developed an online list of Web sites related to the subject of this book. This site is updated regularly. Please use this link to access the list:

http://www.rosenlinks.com/faq/fin

Bellenir, Karen. *Debt Information for Teens.* Detroit, MI:
Omnigraphics, 2007.

Blatt, Jessica, and Variny Paladino. *The Teen Girl's Gotta-
Have-It Guide to Money.* New York, NY: Watson-Guptill
Publications, 2008.

Burleson, Kimberly Spinks, and Robyn Collins. *Prepare to
Be a Teen Millionaire.* Deerfield Beach, FL: Health
Communications, 2008.

Clark, Teri B. *The Complete Personal Finance Handbook.*
Ocala, FL: Atlantic Publishing Group, 2007.

Cribb, Joe. *Money.* New York, NY: DK Eyewitness Books, 2005.

Deering, Kathryn R. *Cash and Credit Information for Teens.*
Detroit, MI: Omnigraphics, 2005.

Deering, Kathryn R. *Savings and Investment Information for
Teens.* Detroit, MI: Omnigraphics, 2005.

Lordan, Meredith. *The World Bank and the International
Monetary Fund.* New York, NY: Chelsea House, 2008.

McKay, Lucia. *Budgeting and Banking Math.* Costa Mesa,
CA: Saddleback Educational Publishing, 2005.

Sander, Jennifer Basye, and Peter Sander. *The Pocket Idiot's
Guide to Living on a Budget.* New York, NY: Alpha
Books, 2005.

Seitchek, Cara. *A Young Adult's Guide to Money.* Redondo
Beach, CA: Money Matters Magazine, 2009.

Bibliography

Bodnar, Janet. "Scare Teens Away from Credit?" *Kiplinger's Money Smart Kids*, October 25, 2006. Retrieved February 2, 2010 (http://www.kiplinger.com/columns/drt/archive/2006/dt061025.html).

Cohen, Russell. "Plastic Power: If You've Got a Credit Card, Here's How to Use It Wisely and Avoid Going into Debt." *Scholastic Choices*, Vol. 22, No. 2, October, 2006, p. 25.

Davis, Mark. "Protections, Pitfalls Ahead in Plastic Use." *Kansas City Star*, January 24, 2010, p. A1, A10.

Dolan Media Newswires. "2006 Junior Achievement Interprise Poll: Working Teens Save for College." *New Orleans CityBusiness*, May 22, 2006.

Fieg, Nancy. "Today's Teen: Braces, Prom, and Credit Histories," *Community Banker*, Vol. 14, No. 12, December 2005, p. 60.

Fisher, Sarah Young, and Susan Shelly. *The Complete Idiot's Guide to Personal Finance in Your 20s and 30s*. New York, NY: Alpha Books, 2009.

Gitman, Lawrence J., and Michael D. Joehnk. *Personal Financial Planning*. Mason, OH: South-Western Cengage Learning, 2008.

Gorman, Danielle. "Mulling Opportunity, Risk in the Teen Card Market." *American Banker*, Vol. 173, No. 158, August 15, 2008, p. 7.

H&R Block. "Tax Tips for Teens: Top Five Things to Know to 'Get Yours.'" Retrieved February 20, 2010 (http://www.hrblock.com).

Jepson, Kevin. "AYSOS? NVM the F2F, TXT MSG Banking Deployed by 2 CUs to Target Teens." *Credit Union Journal*, Vol. 11, No. 42, October 22, 2007, p. 24.

Kaplan, Julee, and Rosemary Feitelberg. "Teens Aim for Recession-Chic Prom Season." *WWD*, Vol. 197, No. 91, April 30, 2009, p. 10.

Kiplinger Washington editors. *Kiplinger's Practical Guide to Your Money*. New York, NY: Kaplan Publishing, 2008.

Lewis, Holden. "Online Banking: E-valuating the Virtual Alternative." Retrieved February 2, 2010 (http://www.bankrate.com).

Morris, Mavis, and Tania Sanchez. *The Standard & Poor's Guide to Understanding Personal Finance*. New York, NY: Lightbulb Press, 2006.

Opdyke, Jeff D. *The Wall Street Journal Complete Personal Finance Guidebook*. New York, NY: Crown Publishing Group, 2006.

Stewart, Deb. "Say Hello to Mobile Banking." *ABA Bank Marketing*, Vol. 41, No. 5, June, 2009, p. 16.

Tyson, Eric. *Personal Finance for Dummies*. Hoboken, NJ: Wiley, 2006.

Weekly Reader Corp. "Saving Grace." *Current Health* 2, Vol. 32, No. 8, April–May 2006, p. 5.

Index

About the Author

Mary-Lane Kamberg is a professional writer who has written extensively on business topics for several magazines and writes nonfiction for children and teens. Kamberg recently cashed in some twenty-year U.S. Savings Bonds and got back twice the money that she paid for them.

Photo Credits

Cover Michael Krasowitz/Taxi/Getty Images; p. 5 Jupiter Images/ Comstock/Thinkstock; pp. 8–9 Celia Peterson/arabianEye/ Getty Images; pp. 11, 36 Shutterstock; p. 14 Romilly Lockyer/ The Image Bank/Getty Images; p. 17 Mario Tama/Getty Images; p. 20 © AP Images; p. 23 Tim Matsui/Workbook Stock/ Getty Images; pp. 26–27 Marc Romanelli/Workbook Stock/Getty Images; p. 29 © Courtesy of Equifax; p. 33 Robert Giroux/MCT/ Newscom; p. 39 Mark Elias/Bloomberg via Getty Images; p. 43 Banana Stock/Thinkstock; p. 44–45 Debbie Egan-Chin/ NY Daily News Archive via Getty Images; p. 48 © Bryan Smith/Zuma Press.

Designer: Evelyn Horovicz; Editor: Bethany Bryan; Photo Researcher: Marty Levick